The

THE
American
BLUE BOOK

A guide to the districts in America where Kamala Harris received 80% or more votes in the Presidential Election of 2024

Written and Edited by

Elizabeth Whitney

A Tomales Bay Times Publication

For my granddaughters, Luna and Evangeline. It's gonna be OK.

Published by Tomales Bay Times Publications
P.O. Box 894, Point Reyes Station, CA 94956
www.tomalesbaytimes.com

Cover design and illustrations: Susan Neri
Book design and typography: Owen Gump
Printed and bound in the USA by
EditionOne Books, Richmond, CA

ISBN: 979-8-218-61987-9

Contents

Introduction: The Bluest of the Blue

The American Blue Book is a guide to the imagination. It's not to be confused with conventional guide books. I have not yet been to most of the places listed here. Except for the California chapter which I wrote from memory, the facts chosen for the entries were entirely sourced from Wikipedia, Britannica and relevant websites. I chose details I liked and wove them together to create the entries.

When I say, "Guide to the imagination," I am asking readers of this guidebook to imagine each of these places as sharing strong common qualities and strengths. If we further imagine the 80%ers as a collective within America, what are those qualities and how can they be transformed into the type of political activism that these times require?

My home is in Marin County, California. Marin County voted the Bluest of the Blue in California.

Learning that fact produced a very good feeling in the grim aftermath of the election. Our tiny rural precincts were well over 80%, helping nudge Marin over the 80% threshold. Feeling inspired, I then went on an Internet quest to see where else in America I would find 80% districts. I was curious: What qualities in these geographical units made them 80% plus Kamala Harris strongholds?

My source was whatever map of voting districts showed up in my search. Some states tabulate by county, some by city and some by township. I may have missed pockets within larger districts that were 80%; we can always add on later! (Shout out to Berkeley at 89.8%, Oakland at 88% and Detroit at 89.7%.)

These 44 places share many themes that unite us and, as you read about them, you may sense what we have in common. For one thing there aren't a lot of people around us who wanted what was offered by the opposing candidate. During the campaign, I never felt I had to watch my words in case I triggered a challenge. I can write letters to the editor, and I won't draw scathing responses, and I can be as political as I want and not experience blow back. It feels safe here to be me.

The day after the election there was no sign of crowing from supporters of the winning candidate. Instead, it was an unspoken day of mourning. People were withdrawn and sad and apprehensive. Blessed by an unexpected change of plans, I was able to take off for a week of introversion and backcountry driving in far northern California. My mission was exploring the historic dam removals on the Klamath River. I needed a journey with a positive purpose.

My medicine was seeing the river running free and healthy, thanks to a beautiful collaboration with Native tribes, young people and restoration experts. I found the dirt road that followed the river, and I meandered along with it, leaving the human world of push and pull, argue and react, blame and criticize far behind. I was looking at the biggest dam removal project in the world, and it was good.

Many of these 44 districts have helped restore their environments with local activism. Many of them have championed the rights of humans who have suffered injustice and acknowledged their own dark legacies. Many of them offer sanctuary to the non-conformists and celebrate the richness of diversity in all its flavors. Many of them, particularly in New England, honor the deep roots of the American Revolution and the valiant struggle to overcome a tyrannical regime. The stages of resistance that led to the Revolution are embedded in the land, honored through the heroes whose names are everywhere and whose legends are revered.

Thomas Paine's famous pamphlet *Common Sense* written in 1776 and distributed widely throughout the colonies (500,000 copies were eventually printed) included this assessment of the tyrant the colonists were rebelling against: *"Men who look upon themselves born to reign, and others to obey, soon grow insolent. Selected from the rest of mankind, their minds are early poisoned by importance. The world they act in differs so materially from the world at large that they have but little opportunity of knowing its true interests. When they succeed in the government, they are frequently the most ignorant and unfit of any throughout the dominions."*

We have been here before and we are here again. The first American Revolution brought together rebel spirits and intellectuals, fighters and thinkers, strategists and dreamers. We are still those people. I am committed to non-violent activism, and my personal experience shows me that it is more powerful than violence. It was the moral courage of non-violent activists in the Civil Rights movement that inspired and awakened me as a teenager. That word "woke" is real to me. When a devotee saw the golden radiance around the Buddha, he asked if he was a god. His answer: "I am awake." That is the high road we are called to walk.

The second American Revolution is upon us. We are going to need our imaginations to counter and undo the terrible harm that is unfolding. If we react with violence against persons or property, in word or action, we invite escalation. The spiritual warrior fights the inner enemy, the wish to escape into a false reality of avoidance. We all need to find our place in what is coming, to protect others, to disobey obscene rules, to stand shoulder to shoulder with those who are unjustly targeted. When we are isolated, we feel vulnerable and outnumbered. When we are the 80%, we are empowered.

The purpose of *The American Blue Book* is to inspire the 80% to identify as a vanguard in the resistance movement against the current tyranny. If you live in one of these districts, begin the grassroots movement and network with your closest communities. You have the freedom to operate with no countervailing winds against you. You have powerful centers of learning in your districts, institutions of science, technology and religious faith. Among you are the cream of the creatives in every art form. You celebrate profound legacies of human achievement in every imaginable arena. Your community efforts manifest the values we all share as descendants of the first American Revolution. You are free to serve and inspire in any way you choose, drawing from your deep inner reserves and your community. This is our time and our destiny, and we are the force.

District of Columbia
92.5% Blue

In 1790 the U.S. Congress established a 100-square-mile territory to serve as the permanent seat of the federal government. The nation's capital was named in honor of George Washington, and the name Columbia, a feminine form of Columbus, was given to the district. Columbia was a poetic name for the United States commonly used at that time. Designed in 1791 by Pierre Charles L'Enfant, a French army engineer who fought in the American Revolution, the city is divided into quadrants, which are centered around the Capitol Building. Congress held its first session there on November 17, 1800. Many government buildings, monuments, and museums along the National Mall and surrounding areas are inspired by classical Roman and Greek architecture. They feature large pediments, domes, columns and heavy stone walls. Visitors to Washington, D.C. are drawn to a dizzying range of attractions: iconic monuments and memorials, the Capitol Building, the Supreme Court and the White House, and formidable museums of science, art and history. Washingtonisaplanned city and many of these structures sit in beautiful natural settings enhancing their symbolic importance to the nation.

Rock Creek Park bisects the city through a stream valley in a 1,754 acre urban forest, which extends 9.3 miles. Established in 1890, it is the country's fourth oldest national park and is home to a variety of plant and animal species, including raccoon, deer, owls, and coyotes. The National Zoological Park occupies about 160 acres of Rock Creek Park. Among the zoo's main attractions are the panda bears, on long term loan from China. The National Mall is a park near downtown Washington that stretches nearly two miles from the Lincoln Memorial to the United States Capitol. The mall often hosts political protests, concerts, festivals, and presidential inaugurations.

Washington, DC: Pop. 689,545 92.5%

KH: 294,185 DT: 21,076 [6.6%]

Washington, famously, is a place of history and reflection on the American experience from its Revolution to the present. Memorials dedicated to its most influential presidents, somber memorials of wars where American soldiers served, and grand houses of government are familiar images to most Americans. Epic moments, such as the 1963 March on Washington for Jobs and Freedom, show Washington as a backdrop to turning points in history. The Capitol Buildings (which included the Supreme Court and the Library of Congress) and the White House were sacked, looted and burned in 1814 by the British in the War of 1812, largely due to their symbolic status. The powerful images of the January 6, 2021, attack on the Capitol by disgruntled and inflamed right wing supporters of the loser of the 2020 presidential election held the nation riveted in disbelief and shock for hours. Unfortunately, the conflict still resonates to this day.

Massachusetts
61.6% Blue

The history of Massachusetts is synonymous with American history, with many epic events in its locales etched forever in the American imagination. It was a site of early English colonization when the Plymouth Colony was founded in 1620 by the Pilgrims of the Mayflower. In the late 18th century, Boston became known as the "Cradle of Liberty" for the agitation there that later led to the American Revolution. Massachusetts natives Samuel Adams, John Adams, and John Hancock were leaders who would become important figures in the Revolution. On December 16, 1773, when a tea ship of the East India Company was planning to land taxed tea in Boston, a group of local men known as the Sons of Liberty sneaked onto the boat the night before and dumped all the tea into the harbor, an act known as the Boston Tea Party. Paul Revere's midnight ride was an alert given to Minutemen in the Province of Massachusetts Bay by local patriots on the night of April 18, 1775, warning them of the approach of British Army troops prior to the battles of Lexington and Concord. In 1786, Shay's Rebellion, a populist revolt led by disaffected American Revolutionary War veterans, influenced the Constitutional Convention. Before the Civil War, the state was a center for the abolitionist, temperance, and transcendentalist movements.

Today, Massachusetts is the second wealthiest state in the U.S. with the state's wealthiest towns located in the Boston suburbs. Many summer communities are located along the shores of Cape Cod where second-home owners vacation.

Massachusetts has a reputation for social and political progressivism; it is the only U.S. state with a right to shelter law, and in 2004 it was the first U.S. state to legally recognize same-sex marriage. Harvard University in Cambridge is the oldest institution of higher learning in the United States, with the largest financial endowment of any university in the world.

The following 17 townships voted 80% or more for Kamala Harris:

Provincetown: 91.5%
Amherst: 88%
Cambridge: 87.8%
Aquinnah: 87.6%
Pelham: 87.4%
Northampton: 85.4%
Brookline: 84.9%
Chilmark: 84.3%
Somerville: 84.6%
Williamstown: 83.8%
Leverett: 83.6%
Arlington: 82.1%
Stockbridge: 82%
Lincoln: 82%
Concord: 81.8%
Monterey: 81.3%
West Tisbury: 80.6%

Provincetown: Pop. 3,664 91.5%

KH: 2,429 DT: 191 [7.2%]

In 1620, the sailing ship Mayflower, carrying Separatists from the Church of England in their search for religious tolerance, landed on Cape Cod at what is now Provincetown. Today, Provincetown is a coastal resort town on the tip of Cape Cod in Barnstable County, still in its way protecting those in search of freedom from intimidation. It is America's oldest continuous art colony, with a flourishing contemporary art scene of galleries, museums and art houses. Provincetown Theater is the "Birthplace of modern theater." It has a strong LGBTQ culture and presence, and its summer activities are frequently centered around festivals and Pride events. Its tourist promotion invites visitors to join the Portuguese Festival, Frolic Weekend, Carnival, Book Festival, Women's Week, spas, and shopping. Many summer tourists and visitors swell the population. Meanwhile, beaches and hiking trails invite appreciation for Provincetown's surrounding natural beauty in the expansive Cape Cod National Seashore.

Amherst: Pop. 39,263 88%

KH: 9,316 DT: 889 [8.4%]

Amherst is known for bookishness, artsiness, local food obsession, openness, tolerance, and beauty. Located in the lovely Pioneer Valley of western Massachusetts, Amherst is a vibrant, intellectual hub. Three prestigious colleges call Amherst home: Amherst College, Hampshire College, and the University of Massachusetts at Amherst. The youthful, lively downtown boasts an independent movie theater, diverse restaurants, and a handful of coffee shops, museums, art galleries, and bookstores set against the backdrop of historical architecture and blooming flower gardens. The character of Amherst is rooted in its colorful and abundant agricultural landscape. Amherst's farmland grounds and balances the town's otherwise largely academic pursuits, and, as its website states, "Amherst is profoundly grateful to our farmland and farmers for providing this sustenance and inspiration for our lives."

Cambridge: Pop. 119,008 **87.8%**

KH: 43,690 **DT: 4,159 [8.3%]**

Cambridge was founded in 1630 and named in honor of the University of Cambridge in England, which was an important center of the Puritan theology embraced by the town's founders. It is located on the Charles River across from Boston. Harvard University, founded in 1636, is the oldest university in the U.S. It is steeped in history from the time of the Puritans through the tide of immigration from Europe bringing Irish immigrants from the Potato Famine followed by immigrants from Italy, Portugal, and Poland, plus French Canadians and Russian Jews. One-fourth of the city's residents are college students. Radcliffe, MIT, and the Smithsonian Center of Astrophysics are all located in Cambridge.

It honors a deep literary culture. *The Cambridge History of English and American Literature,* published in the early 20th Century, is considered the most important work of literary history ever published. Its 11,000 entries fill 303 pages, encompassing a wide selection of writing from orators, humorists, poets, columnists, religious leaders, economists, Native Americans, song writers, and even non-English writing, such as Yiddish and Creole. Eight U.S. Presidents were Harvard graduates: John Adams, John Quincy Adams, Rutherford B. Hayes, Theodore Roosevelt, Franklin Delano Roosevelt, John F. Kennedy, George W. Bush, and Barack Obama.

Aquinnah: Pop. 439 **87.6%**

KH: 304 **DT: 37 [10%]**

Aquinnah is known for its beautiful clay cliffs and natural serenity, as well as its historical importance to the native Wampanoag people. Aquinnah is celebrated as a center of Wampanoag culture and a center of pride and tradition among members of the federally recognized Wampanoag Tribe of Gay Head. They comprise approximately one-third of the town's voters and are one of two federally recognized tribes of Wampanoag people in Massachusetts. This area is one of the earliest sites of whaling, with the Wampanoag harpooning their catch long before commercial whaling became the major maritime industry of Martha's Vineyard. In 1997, by a popular vote of 79 to 21, the town changed its name to *Aquinnah,* Wampanoag for "land under the hill." Throughout the town's history, a Wampanoag community has been among its residents. The people gained federal recognition in 1987 and control sovereign tribal lands within the town boundaries.

Pelham: Pop. 1,280 **87.4%**

KH: 748 **DT: 88 [10.3%]**

Pelham describes itself as a "small, pleasant town in central Massachusetts." Founded in 1654, it is the oldest town in Westchester County. The Old Town Hall, built in 1743, is claimed to be the oldest continuously used town hall in the United States. The town lies along the hills which divide the Pioneer Valley along the Connecticut River to the west from the Quabbin Valley to the east. The brooks in town flow in two directions; those in the eastern third of town drain towards the Quabbin, with the western brooks draining towards the Connecticut River. The town has several forests, some of which are protected; these include Cadwell Memorial Forest, Buffam Falls Conservation Area and the Quabbin lands. Home to many retired people and commuters, the school district is Pelham's largest employer.

Northampton: Pop. 29,327 85.4%

KH: 14,477 DT: 1,800 [10.6%]

Originally known as *Nonotuck*, an Algonquian word meaning "middle of the river," Northampton was settled in 1654 and named for Northampton, England. Located on the Connecticut River in Hampshire County, today Northampton is known as an academic, artistic, musical, and countercultural hub. It features a large politically liberal community along with numerous alternative health and intellectual organizations. Nicknamed "Paradise City," Northampton was identified as "The most politically liberal medium-sized city in the U.S." [ePodunk website]. It is LGBTQ friendly and has five times the national average of same sex unmarried households. Smith College was founded in Northampton in 1871 and is the largest of the Seven Sisters colleges. Sojourner Truth arrived in Florence (a village of Northampton) in 1843, joining a utopian community dedicated to equality and justice. She and many of the country's important abolitionists helped establish Florence as a center of antislavery resistance. Several Florence homes were stops on the Underground Railroad. The city is also home to the oldest continuously running agricultural fair in the United States, held each September.

Brookline: Pop. 63, 373 **84.9%**

KH: 23,710 **DT: 3,497 [12.5%]**

Brookline is in Norfolk County within the greater Boston metropolitan area. Originally known as the Hamlet of Muddy River, it was settled in 1638 and incorporated in 1703. It has a history of discriminatory zoning and thus has a low percentage (2.5%) of Blacks and a disproportionately wealthy population. It also has a large Irish American presence. John F. Kennedy and his brother Robert Kennedy were born in Brookline; JFK lived there until the age of 10. Old records note its "Pleasant and verdant environment." It is the cultural hub of the Jewish community of Greater Boston. The Puppet Showplace Theater in Brookline is New England's center for puppetry arts and a treasured cultural institution. Brookline residents were among the first in history to propose extending voting rights to women in the gubernatorial campaign of Benjamin F. Butler in 1882.

Chilmark: Pop. 1,227 84.3%

KH: 770 DT: 123 [13.%]

Chilmark is a charming town on the island of Martha's Vineyard, where you can enjoy the rural scenery, the fishing culture, and the history of the region. Visitors can explore the town's hilly terrain and admire the views from the island's highest elevation. On a visit to the fishing village of Menemsha, the agenda is watching boats come and go, sampling the fresh seafood, and witnessing the spectacular sunsets. The sandy beaches of Menemsha and Lucy Vincent offer swimming, surfing, and sunbathing. The town's unique heritage includes the fact that it was once home to a large deaf community and the first English settlement on the island.

The Chilmark Community Church sponsors the popular Chilmark Flea Market during the summer and is the oldest outdoor venue on the island. The 50 year old "Flea" has evolved into a market like no other with high quality handmade items from Vineyard artists and craftsmen, antiques, imports, collectibles and vintage finds.

Somerville: Pop. 80,636 84.6%

KH: 33,636 DT: 4,512 [11.5%]

Somerville, in Middlesex County, is located two miles north of Boston on the Mystic River. Occupying slightly over four square miles, it is the most densely populated community in New England and one of the most ethnically diverse cities in the nation. It is the home of Tufts University, which, with Harvard and MIT, make up the "Brain Power Triangle." After New York City, Somerville has more artists per capita than any other U.S. city. The Mystic River is one of the Commonwealth's best protected watercourses; almost the entirety of the riverbank is open to the public. The city went through a gentrification period in the 1990s drawing an influx of artists to the area and gaining a reputation as an active arts community. Nowadays lobbying by grassroots organizations is attempting to revive and preserve Somerville's "small-town" neighborhood environments by supporting local business, public transit and gardens.

Williamstown: Pop. 7,510 **83.8%**

KH: 3,006 **DT: 495 [13.8%]**

Williamstown, in the northwest corner of the Commonwealth of Massachusetts, borders Vermont to the north and New York to the west in Berkshire County. It is home to Williams College, the Clark Art Institute and the Tony-awarded Williamstown Theatre Festival. For its unique blend of small town charm and world class culture, Williamstown is a Massachusetts Cultural District, supporting arts, humanities, and science organizations. It is also a year-round vacation site with recreational tourism in the nearby Berkshires and along the Hoosic River.

Leverett: Pop. 7,510 83.6%

KH: 1,079 DT: 160 [12.4%]

Leverett, in Franklin County, is neighbor to the Five College area of Amherst, Hampshire, Smith, Mt. Holyoke and the University of Massachusetts. Its diverse population is a rich mixture of teachers, students, farmers, lumbermen, gardeners, artists, and professionals in the areas of medicine, law, and telecommunications.

Leverett is unusually rich in scenic beauty. Rattlesnake Gutter Road, in the heart of the town, is a two mile road through a boulder-filled glacial ravine, bordered by Brushy Mountain. The Sawmill River cascades over rocks in Moore's Corner emptying into Leverett Pond in the center of town, a place of quiet beauty. The first Peace Pagoda in the U.S. sits majestically at the top of Cave Hill.

Arlington: Pop. 45,430 **82.1%**

KH: 22,399 **DT: 4,219 [15%]**

Arlington is a suburb of Boston in Middlesex County that is popular for its wildlife and nature, historic lore, and tourism. It offers a glimpse into the history and culture of Massachusetts and has a vibrant arts scene, with two theaters, several museums, and local artists showcasing their work. Old Schwamb Mill is the oldest continuously operated mill site in the nation. For nature lovers, Arlington has plenty of parks and open spaces, such as the Mystic Lakes, the Minuteman Bikeway, and the Mill Brook.

Stockbridge: Pop. 1,984 **82%**

KH: 1,073 **DT: 213 [16%]**

Stockbridge is a charming village in the heart of the Berkshires, a scenic region of western Massachusetts. Known for its most famous resident, artist Norman Rockwell, the town welcomes you to walk down Main Street as he painted it and step back in time. Stroll along and explore the boutiques, art galleries, and specialty food shops; tour exquisite examples of Gilded Age architecture and gardens; and venture just a little way from downtown to find lovely nature preserves and walking paths. Tanglewood is the famed summer home of the Boston Symphony Orchestra and its training academy, the Tanglewood Music Center, as well as the Boston Pops. It's also the year-round home of the Tanglewood Learning Institute. In a typical summer, Tanglewood welcomes more than 350,000 visitors to performances, recitals, and seminars across 500 acres nestled between Lenox and Stockbridge.

Lincoln: Pop. 6,890 **82%**

KH: 3,258 **DT: 638 [16%]**

Located about 20 miles west of Boston in Middlesex County, Lincoln offers a quiet town feel, beautiful historic homes, museums, and 70 miles of trails through conservation land. The town's understated feel attracts artists, doctors, writers, conservationists, entrepreneurs and CEOs alike. Lincoln has a large amount of colonial history; a substantial portion of the first battle of the Revolutionary War, the Battle of Lexington and Concord, was fought in Lincoln. The two-acre zoning law gives the town a rural feel, and the many ultra-contemporary homes have been tastefully constructed to coexist peacefully with the town's historic feel.

Concord: Pop. 18,119 81.8%

KH: 9,588 DT: 1,924 [16.4%]

Concord, in Middlesex County, lies along the Concord River, 20 miles northwest of Boston. It was the epicenter of two revolutions. The American War of Independence began here on April 19, 1775, and by the middle of the 19th Century the town was the breeding ground for a second revolution: the spiritual, literary and intellectual movement that became known as Transcendentalism. During the 19th century, Concord was a noted cultural center, being the home of Ralph Waldo Emerson, the naturalist Henry David Thoreau, the sculptor Daniel Chester French, and the authors Nathaniel Hawthorne and Louisa May Alcott, all buried in Sleepy Hollow Cemetery. The "Shot heard round the world" refers to the opening shot of the battles of Lexington and Concord on April 19, 1775, which sparked the American Revolutionary War and led to the creation of the United States. It originates from the opening stanza of Emerson's 1837 poem *Concord Hymn*:

By the rude bridge that arched the flood,
Their flag to April's breeze unfurled,
Here once the embattled farmers stood
And fired the shot heard round the world.

The Concord Summer School of Philosophy, founded by A. Branson Alcott (father of Louisa May), met there from 1879 to 1888. The 20th century composer Charles Ives wrote his *Concord Sonata* as a series of impressionistic portraits of literary figures associated with the town.

Concord maintains a lively literary culture to this day; notable authors who have called the town home in recent years include Doris Kearns Goodwin, Alan Lightman, Robert B. Parker, and Gregory Maguire. In 1850 Ephraim Bull perfected the Concord grape, marking the beginning of commercial cultivation of table grapes in the United States; the original vine still grows at his home on Lexington Road.

Monterey: Pop. 1,071 **81.3%**

KH: 482 **DT: 95 [16%]**

Monterey lies in the southern end of the Berkshires, at the headwaters of the Konkapot River in Berkshire County. The town was mostly known for its sawmills, but today it is a rural community, known more for its recreational areas. Surrounded by lakes, streams, and forests, Monterey offers a peaceful retreat from the hustle and bustle of the city—a hidden gem of the Berkshires. Visitors explore the trails and wildlife of Beartown State Forest or relax by the shore of Lake Garfield. The Roadside Store & Cafe advertises "A taste of local culture and cuisine, where you can savor homemade soups, sandwiches, and pies."

West Tisbury: Pop: 3,564 80.6%

KH: 1,757 DT: 367 [16.8%]

West Tisbury is a charming town on Martha's Vineyard in Dukes County, off the Massachusetts coast. Historically, it was the agricultural heartland of the island. West Tisbury covers 34 square miles, with a small full time population—a number that grows to several times that in the summer. Visitors can explore the old English settlement, the historic lumberyard, and the cranberry bog, or relax on the sandy beaches of Lambert's Cove and Makonikey. West Tisbury offers a peaceful escape from the busy down-island towns, with its rolling hills, lush forests, and quaint farms. The town prides itself on retaining a rural atmosphere and a neighborly sense of community.

Vermont
64.4% Blue

In 1774, following an excessive tax upon the colonies, the area now known as Vermont revolted. Calling themselves the Green Mountain Boys, rebels rampaged throughout the north, killing redcoats and taking forts. The people of the north supported the cause and rallied en masse following heavier taxing and quartering in early 1776. By 1777 the new Republic of the Green Mountains issued a Declaration of Independence, penned by Benjamin Franklin and John Adams. The Vermont Constitution was the first written constitution in North America to ban adult slavery, stating that male slaves become free at the age of 21 and females at 18. It provided for universal adult male suffrage and established a public school system. Vermonters also provided refuge for escaped slaves fleeing to Canada, as part of the Underground Railroad. The Vermont Republic functioned for 14 years before being admitted to the United States, the first state to enter the Union after the original 13 states.

Every April, hundreds of Vermont students in grades 5 through 12 and homeschool students ages 10 to 18 share their learning at the annual Vermont History Day state contest. At the state contest, students present their claims to local historians, educators, and other professionals who participate as judges.

Known for its progressivism, Vermont was one of the first states in the U.S. to recognize same-sex civil unions and marriage.It is one of the least religious and least racially and ethnically diverse states. It has the highest proportion of renewable electricity generation (99.9%). Dairy, forestry, and wine are important sectors in the state's agricultural economy, and Vermont produces approximately 50% of the nation's maple syrup.

The following 11 townships, including the largest (Burlington) and smallest (Landgrove), voted 80% or more for Kamala Harris:

Norwich: 90.5%
Montpelier City: 86.8%
Burlington: 85.1%
Warren: 84.5%
Fayston: 82.9%
Landgrove: 82.5%
Strafford 81.6%
Waitsfield: 81.5%
Weybridge: 81.%
Shelburne: 81%
South Burlington: 80.0%

Norwich: Pop. 3,639 90.5%

KH: 2,234 DT: 193 [7.8%]

Located in Windsor County, Norwich is home to some of Vermont's wealthiest residents. The municipality is a commuter town for nearby Hanover, New Hampshire, home of Dartmouth College. Norwich lies on the western bank of the Connecticut River, which forms Vermont's boundary with New Hampshire, opposite its companion town, Hanover. The Ledyard Bridge connects the two towns. The Montshire Museum of Science and King Arthur Baking Company are in Norwich.

Montpelier City: Pop. 7,964 86.8%

KH: 4,359 DT: 491 [9.8%]

Montpelier is the state capital and the county seat of Washington County. The site of Vermont's state government, it is the least populous state capital in the United States. Before European settlement in the region, the Abenaki and their ancestors were the stewards of the valley and hills that today correspond to the city of Montpelier. Montpelier's location along the Winooski River near the mouths of the Dog River and the North Branch meant that it likely served as a travel corridor for Native people for at least 11,000 years. Beginning about 1,000 CE, Native people began to practice intensive agriculture in Vermont. Surviving Abenaki descendants have emerged from hiding in recent decades to reclaim their culture and history. Today, there are four State-recognized Abenaki tribes.

"Montpelier's reputation as a good food haven was sealed in 1996 when the planning commission turned down an application from McDonald's to open a downtown restaurant on State Street. The city is the only state capital without a McDonald's, although there is one nearby in Berlin. While the city adapts to global changes and local concerns, it tries to retain the advantages, opportunities, and pleasures of small-scale living."

[Essay and research by Paul A. Carnahan, Librarian, Vermont Historical Society]

Burlington: Pop. 44,455 **85.1%**

KH: 17,414 **DT: 2,222 [10.9%]**

Burlington is the most populous city in the state of Vermont and the seat of Chittenden County. It is the least populous city in the 50 U.S. states to be the most populous city in its state. Burlington is situated on the eastern shore of Lake Champlain, north of Shelburne Bay. Bernie Sanders was mayor of Burlington from 1981-1989. His administration was the first socialist one in New England since the mayoralty of Jasper McLevy in Bridgeport CT (1933-1957). Vermont's largest city is also its cultural hub: Burlington is abuzz with music, history and opportunities for outdoor exploring. The scenic Burlington Bike Path traverses the city's once-industrial waterfront, now home to an independent craft brewery. Other attractions are the Shelburne Museum, Huntington's Green Mountain Audubon Center and hiking in bird-friendly forests where maple syrup is produced each spring over roaring wood fires. Also near Burlington is the Ben & Jerry's factory in Waterbury where aficionados can taste their way through the company's ice cream canon.

Warren: Pop. 1,982 **84.5%**

KH: 1,020 **DT: 150 [12%]**

The history of Warren is like many upland Vermont towns with early development focused on agriculture, timber cutting, and small water-powered industries. The Mad River Valley has several such towns, but Warren has the most developed mill economy. It is set between the two ranges of the Green Mountains, with approximately 25% of the township within the boundaries of the federal Green Mountain National Forest. Sugarbush Resort is a local ski resort in the town. The Long Trail, a trail running from the border with Massachusetts to the Canada—U.S. border traverses the town.

Fayston: Pop. 1,419 **82.9%**

KH: 768 **DT: 139 [15%]**

Fayston is a rural community within Vermont's Mad River Valley that offers recreational, business and lifestyle opportunities. Home to Sugarbush's Mount Ellen and Mad River Glen ski areas, the town offers ski related facilities and services. Its picturesque community is also a favorite for backcountry skiing and snowshoeing, hiking, cycling, paddling, hunting and snowmobiling. It has numerous restaurants and lodging establishments and an active historical society.

"It's much more than a ski community. It was a farming community before the ski world got here, and it's still kind of a working landscape of farms, artisans, shops, restaurants and the ski resorts."

[Local resident and inn owner]

Landgrove: Pop. 173 82.5%

KH: 94 DT: 15 [13.2%]

Landgrove, Vermont, is a town in Bennington County, located northwest of Londonderry, southwest of Weston, and northeast of Peru. It is a secluded, quiet area, hidden among the beautiful scenery of the surrounding Green Mountains. There is no traffic, no stores, and best of all, no noise...just forest, meadows, dirt roads, and quiet beauty. Artists come from far and wide to sketch or paint the barns, fields, and mountains that surround the valley. During the warmer months, activities in the area include hiking, biking, or swimming in nearby Hapgood Pond. During the winter, skiing can be found at nearby Bromley Mountain and Magic Mountain.

Waitsfield: Pop. 1,894 **81.5%**

KH: 989 **DT: 196 [16.15%]**

Waitsfield sits in the heart of the Mad River Valley in Washington County. It is surrounded by spectacular natural beauty, including the Green Mountains and the Mad River. This is a place where the local traditions of community, conservation, recreation, agriculture, commerce, and civic engagement continue to be valued. The town's economy is largely supported by two nearby ski resorts, Sugarbush Resort and Mad River Glen. A long-running Christmas ad for Miller High Life beer was filmed in Waitsfield in 1980. Lawson's Finest Liquids features a taproom that brews award-winning beers with local ingredients.

Weybridge: Pop. 830 81%

KH: 482 DT: 90 [15.5%]

Weybridge is located in central Addison County in the Champlain Valley. Otter Creek weaves through the town on its way to Lake Champlain. Weybridge is home to the University of Vermont Morgan Horse Farm and Monument Farms Dairy. Colonel Joseph Battell began breeding Morgans on his farm in Weybridge in the late 1870s. His intense interest in preserving and promoting America's first breed of horse saved the Morgan from extinction. Chartered in 1761 by a hardy crew from Connecticut, Weybridge continues its traditions of farming, waterpower and close community.

Strafford: Pop. 1,102 81.6%

KH: 649 DT: 122 [15.3%]

"We're off the beaten path," says Bob Johnston, a local historian who has lived in Strafford for 15 years. "A resident once described Strafford to me as a 'bubble within a bubble.'" The Strafford Town House is one of the oldest meeting houses in Vermont. It is listed on the National Register of Historic Places and is part of the Strafford Village Historic District. Erected in 1799 by local carpenters, this beautiful structure was built as a place to do public business and served as a meeting house for various religious denominations. Strafford's annual Town Meeting has been held in this building every year since 1801.

The Elizabeth Mine was once a hub of industrial activity, thanks to a pocket of copper ore that was discovered. It was in operation from the 1800s until 1958. It became an EPA Superfund Site in 2001. The cleanup, initiated in 2003, was completed in 2021. Eight acres of toxic wetlands with 15 acres of healthy wetlands were created and reduced the iron load to receiving bodies of water from 800 pounds per day to one-tenth of a pound per day. The Elizabeth Mine tailings impoundment, once capped, was repurposed into a solar field.

Shelburne: Pop. 7,972 **81%**

KH: 4,472 **DT: 915 [17.7%]**

Set on the shores of Lake Champlain in Chittenden County, Shelburne is seven miles south of Burlington. Not only is Shelburne home to Northern New England's largest art and history museum, but its beautiful natural areas, quirky outdoor art, and farm-to-table fare make this one of Vermont's most beloved areas to explore. Three major tourist attractions are the Shelburne Museum, Shelburne Farms, and the Vermont Teddy Bear Company. The town maintains a beach on Lake Champlain with a boat launch and nature park.

South Burlington: Pop. 21,293 80%

KH: 9,974 DT: 2,207 [17.7%]

South Burlington is a principal city of the Burlington metropolitan area and the second largest city in Vermont. The Winooski River runs along its northern edges. It calls itself a city "Where modernity intertwines with a profound appreciation for nature." It is the home of Ben and Jerry's Ice Cream, Vermont's largest mall, the Burlington International Airport and an impressive lineup of cutting edge technologies. According to the personal finance outlet website WalletHub.com, South Burlington was named the safest city in 2024. Some of the reasons cited include having one of the lowest pedestrian fatality rates in the country, the ninth-most EMTs and paramedics per capita, and the lowest unemployment rate in the country, at 1.9%.

Virginia
52.1% Blue

Virginia, named for Elizabeth I, the Virgin Queen, is steeped in history, natural beauty and tradition. The settlement at Jamestown in 1607 is acknowledged as the birthplace of the United States. History and nature make Virginia a leading tourist center. Many beautiful names evoke Virginia's historical significance and natural attractions: Shenandoah, Appalachia, Chesapeake, Appomattox, Allegheny, Rappahannock, and the Blue Ridge Mountains. Mt. Vernon and Monticello, homes of George Washington and Thomas Jefferson, are honored with gracious historic estates. Contemporary historic festivals abound, such as the famed Annual Pony Swim, Auction and Carnival when saltwater cowboys herd and swim wild ponies from Assateague Island to neighboring Chincoteague Island. There are several ballet companies, orchestras, civic choruses, opera and theatre companies, as well as numerous festivals of the arts. Bluegrass and mountain-music festivals are especially popular in the summer months. The federal government is a dominant economic presence in Virginia. Many military institutions lie within the state's boundaries, as well as the headquarters of the Central Intelligence Agency.

These four districts voted 80% or more
for Kamala Harris:

Petersburg: 85.5%
Charlottesville: 83.4%
Richmond: 82%
Falls Church: 80.3%

Petersburgh: Pop. 33,282 85.5%

KH: 11,219 DT: 1,702 [13%]

The majority race in Petersburg is Black, making up 55.3% of residents. The next most common racial group is white at 32.5%. At the time of the American Civil War, Petersburg was the second-largest city in Virginia after the capital, Richmond, and the seventh-largest city in the Confederacy. Petersburg's population had the highest percentage of free Black Americans of any city in the Confederacy and the largest number of free Blacks in the Mid-Atlantic region. In the years after the Civil War, many freedmen migrated to Petersburg, founding numerous churches, businesses and institutions.

Petersburg has endured the trials of the civil rights struggle in all its aspects. Major black churches, such as First Baptist and Gillfield Baptist, formed the moral center of the movement in Petersburg, which gained strength in mid-century and was a center of action. In 1968, following the assassination of Martin Luther King Jr., Petersburg was the first city to designate his birthday as a holiday. In 2023, Governor Glenn Youngkin launched the Partnership for Petersburg initiative with state, local, community, and faith leaders. With support from the Commonwealth's resources,the Partnership's mission is to help Petersburg become one of the best cities to live, work, and raise a family.

Charlottesville: Pop. 44,487 **83.4%**

KH: 19,435 **DT: 3,428 [14.7%]**

Charlottesville is in central Virginia along the Rivanna River. Monticello, Thomas Jefferson's plantation manor, is a few miles from downtown. James Madison and James Monroe also have heritage homes there. History runs deep in this vibrant city, which is also known for music, theater, film, museums, festivals and restaurants. The Downtown Mall is one of the longest pedestrian malls in the US.

Attempts to remove statues of Robert E. Lee and Stonewall Jackson from downtown parks have been the subject of extensive, unresolved litigation. In August 2017, white supremacist groups organized the "Unite the Right" rally to protest the removal of the Lee statue from Lee Park, subsequently renamed Emancipation Park. After the rally, a white nationalist drove a car into protesters, resulting in the death of counter-protester Heather Heyer and causing injuries to 19 others. The incident became national news, and Charlottesville became a symbol of political turbulence nationwide. The city succeeded in the removal of the Lee and Jackson statues on July 10, 2021. A statue of the Lewis and Clark exhibition was also removed when descendants of Sacagawea argued it showed her in an unfavorable light, crouching below the two expedition leaders.

Richmond: Pop. 88,710 **82%**

KH: 88,710 **DT: 17,041 [15%]**

Richmond is the capital city of the Commonwealth of Virginia. During the Revolutionary War, several notable events occurred in the city, including Patrick Henry's "Give me liberty, or give me death!" speech in 1775 at St. John's Church and the passage of the Virginia Statute for Religious Freedom written by Thomas Jefferson. During the American Civil War, Richmond was the capital of the Confederate States of America. In the post-bellum era, the population surged. Freed slaves and their descendants created a thriving African American business community, and the city's historic Jackson Ward became known as the "Wall Street of Black America." Most of the statues honoring Confederate leaders on Monument Avenue were removed during or after the George Floyd protests in 2020. The only statue remaining on Monument Avenue is of Arthur Ashe, the pioneering Black tennis player. A tradition of theater, opera, ballet, film, literature and fine arts are woven into Richmond's rich political history.

Falls Church: Pop. 14,686 80.3%

KH: 7,200 DT: 1,620 [18.1%]

The City of Falls Church is a unique and historic city, located across the Potomac River 10 miles from Washington, DC. It was named after the historic Falls Church prayer house, established as an Episcopal church in 1732. Almost every neighborhood is a treasure of its own with a variety of restaurants and shops that reflect the city's great ethnic and cultural diversity. At 2.11 square miles, Falls Church is the smallest incorporated municipality in the Commonwealth of Virginia and the smallest county-equivalent municipality in the United States. Eden Center is the largest Vietnamese commercial center on the East Coast and the largest Asian mall on North America's East Coast.

"The City of Falls Church acknowledges that, at times in the past, diverse voices and perspectives were often silenced. Today, we are dedicated to being a welcoming and inclusive community—a special place in the heart of Northern Virginia."

[City website]

Connecticut
56.46% Blue

C*onnecticut* is the anglicized spelling of *Quinnetuket*, a Mohegan-Pequot word for "Upon the long tidal river," referring to the Connecticut River that bisects the state and is the longest river in New England. Despite its small size, Connecticut features wide regional variations in its landscape: rolling mountains and horse farms, coastal marshes, beaches, and large scale maritime activities. The state motto is *Qui transtulit sustinet*—"He Who Transplanted Still Sustains"—reflecting the faith of the early colonists. The state tree is the Charter Oak. (It's also called the Nutmeg State, but no one really knows why.) Another motto associated with it is "The Land of Steady Habits." Like much of New England, it is steeped in history and reflects the aesthetics of the early English settlers. Many towns center around a green, surrounded by historical visual icons, such as a white church, a colonial meeting house, or a colonial tavern or inn. These establish a scenic, historical appearance maintained for both historic preservation and tourism.

These are the three cites who voted 80% or more for Kamala Harris:

Bloomfield: 83.8%
Hartford: 81.8%
New Haven: 80.6%

Bloomfield: Pop: 22,235 **83.8%**

KH: 9,692 **DT: 1,760 [15.2%]**

Bloomfield is located in central Connecticut, just 10 minutes west of the state capitol, Hartford. Initially, Bloomfield's economy was agriculturally based, mostly in shade tobacco. It developed as a postwar suburb of Hartford in the 1950s. In the nineteenth century, one of the most lucrative as well as respectable industries in town was the making of cider brandy. Today, Bloomfield's local character varies. While the town's southern and eastern fringes are more densely populated and developed, the northern and western sections maintain a more rural feel with meadows, woods, and some remaining farmland. Its top employer is The Cigna Group, a multinational for-profit managed health care and insurance business associated with a history of controversy.

Hartford: Pop. 11,9626 81.8%

KH: 19,089 DT: 4,271 [18.1%]

Hartford is the capital city of Connecticut and among the oldest cities in the United States. Located in the Connecticut River valley, Hartford has a fascinating history of industrial development and manufacturing. Rifles, sewing machines, typewriters, bicycles and screws were all manufactured in the golden era of Hartford's many major precision manufacturing innovations. Over the years the steady decline of industrialization took a toll on the city, and the population shrank 11 percent during the 1990s. These forces set off a financial crisis which resulted in a near bankruptcy in 2017. A slow comeback seems to be in play. Today, Hartford is known as a center for medical care, research, and education. It is also an international center of the insurance industry and a burgeoning technology hub. The city's strong cultural and educational core includes Trinity College and UConn's Hartford Campus. Many historic sites, museums, art centers, theatres, parks and sports centers remain vibrant and vital. Cultural diversity is celebrated by ethnic festivals and parades and a variety of cuisines. Many famous writers found a home in Hartford, the most being Samuel Clemens who is honored at the Mark Twain home and museum.

New Haven: Pop: 137,173 80.6%

KH: 30,662 DT: 6,626 [17%]

Founded by English Puritans in 1638, New Haven has found itself in the center of ever-evolving themes of American history for 400 years. Yale University, founded in 1701, is the city's top taxpayer and employer. Yale alumni were represented on the Democratic or Republican ticket in virtually every U.S. presidential election since 1972. The presence of the university magnetized many significant social battles mixing town and gown, from the Revolutionary War to the present. However, New Haven's greatest claim to fame may be its pizza, said to be among the best in the country, or even in the world. Though fiercely debated, Louis Lunch restaurant's founder Louis Lassen is credited with inventing the hamburger in 1900. Other inventions associated with New Haven are the submarine, the steamboat, the revolver, the corkscrew, the lollipop and the erector set, giving New Haven the reputation of being a meeting place of the intelligentsia, the inventor and the cuisine of its immigrants. These diverse elements enhance world-class centers for theater, music, art, dance and history as well as a cosmopolitan urban population.

Maryland
63% Blue

As one of the original Thirteen Colonies, Maryland was founded by George Calvert, a Catholic convert who sought to provide a religious haven for Catholics persecuted in England. Today, Maryland is one of the most multicultural states in the country; 50.2% of its population is non-white, the highest percentage of any state on the East Coast. Caribbean-Americans, especially Jamaican Americans, who make up 0.6% of the population, have had a significant influence in its politics and culture. Maryland ranks as one of the best states in the nation for LGBTQ rights. The first person known to identify as a drag queen was William Dorsey Swann, born enslaved in Hancock, Maryland in 1860. Maryland has several historic and renowned private colleges and universities; the most prominent is Johns Hopkins University.

The Chesapeake Bay provides Marylanders with crabs, clams, oysters and rockfish. Maryland has been called "America in Miniature," because so much is packed into its 10,460 square miles of land and water.

The following two counties voted 80% or more
For Kamala Harris:

Prince Georges County: 86.5%
Baltimore: 85.2%

Prince Georges County: Pop. 947,880 86.5%

KH: 347,038 DT: 27,984 [15.5%]

Prince George's County lies in the Atlantic coastal plain and its landscape is formed of gently rolling hills and valleys. There are five key regions to Prince George's County: North County, Central County, Rural Tier, Inner Beltway, and South County. The Inner Beltway communities border neighboring District of Columbia's northeastern and southeastern quadrants. Protected bike trails connect its residents to downtown D.C. The Rural Tier has been the focus of orchestrated efforts by residents and county government to preserve its rural character and environmental integrity. Patuxent River Park is the largest natural preserve and provides public access for birdwatching and viewing its natural waterfront vistas. It is the only portion of Prince George's County to enjoy the Potomac River waterfront. The National Harbor project is a town center and riverside shopping and residential living development on the Potomac.

Prince George's County is the largest and highest income Black-majority county in the US and has a 63% Black population as of 2024. As part of the increasingly liberal D.C. suburbs and a nationwide suburban shift towards the Democrats, Prince George's County is a Democratic stronghold, voting majority-Democratic in every Presidential election but four since 1932.

Baltimore: Pop. 559,266 **85.2%**

KH: 195,109 **DT: 27,984 [12.2%]**

Baltimore is located in north-central Maryland on the Patapsco River, close to where it empties into Chesapeake Bay. Baltimore was designated an independent city by the Constitution of Maryland in 1851. It is the most populous independent city in the US. The Baltimore and Ohio Railroad, the nation's oldest, was built in 1830 and cemented Baltimore's status as a transportation hub, giving producers in the Midwest and Appalachia access to the city's port. After a decline in manufacturing, heavy industry, and restructuring of the rail industry, Baltimore has shifted to a service-oriented economy. Johns Hopkins Hospital and University are the top employers. Lexington Market, founded in 1782 and a center of slave trading, is one of the oldest continuously operating public markets in the United States today.

Baltimore has historically been a working-class port town, sometimes dubbed a "city of neighborhoods" with 72 designated historic districts traditionally occupied by distinct ethnic groups. The port serves over 50 ocean carriers, making nearly 1,800 annual visits. Among all U.S. ports, Baltimore is first in handling automobiles, light trucks, farm and construction machinery; imported forest products, aluminum, and sugar. The port is second in coal exports.

Culturally, Baltimore is rich in architecture, museums of science and art, libraries, theater, music, historic ships, sports, (including Pimlico, home of the Preakness Stakes), and fine seafood restaurants. The Port has been developed into a tourist center with activities for all ages, including the National Aquarium, the largest tourist attraction in the State of Maryland.

California
58.5% Blue

Big, beautiful and brash, the state of California is a major presence in the nation and the world. It is the third-largest state in size (after Alaska and Texas), the largest in population (just under 40 million), and has the fourth largest economy in the world. Culturally, it has left its imprint on the global imagination. In addition to its vast natural resources, abundant parks and legendary beaches, it boasts powerful economic hubs in Hollywood and Silicon Valley and renown tourist attractions.

The Golden State was born in 1848 in the Treaty of Hildalgo, ending the highly controversial Mexican War, the same year that gold was discovered at Sutter's Mill in the Sierra foothills. The subsequent gold rush laid the economic foundation for the future state of

California and embedded in its character themes of fortune hunting, rags-to-riches (and back), and opportunistic fantasies. In the 1960s, California was the mecca of the counter-culture movement that enticed hundreds of thousands of youthful seekers to San Francisco and Los Angeles. A few decades later, the lure was get-rich-quick pipe dreams, and the technology boom was launched in a former agricultural paradise that came to be called Silicon Valley. Ever reeling from its various identities and thorny dilemmas, California is forever a state of mind within the United States, declaring, with its famous motto, *Eureka!*

These two counties voted 80% or more
For Kamala Harris:

Marin: 80.6%
San Francisco: 80.3%

Marin: Pop. 252,660 80.6%

KH: 116,152 DT: 24,054 [16.7%]

Across the Golden Gate Bridge and through the rainbow tunnel lies Marin County, a recreational paradise that serves the San Francisco Bay Area's urban population. Marin County boasts two free national parks and a national monument: the Golden Gate National Recreation Area, the Point Reyes National Seashore, and Muir Woods; six state parks; 10 open space districts, and numerous county parks. From Mt. Tamalpais to vast ocean beaches to the shorelines of San Francisco Bay and Tomales Bay, opportunities abound for locals and visitors alike to tune out and tune in to nature's rhythms. Culturally, Marin is unabashedly affluent and at the same time a counterculture holdout in its rural pockets and a sanctuary for seekers of all stripes. Over the decades since it had the hot tub label attached to it, along with a lot of teasing from East Coast punditry, Marin has stayed steadily at the forefront of the healthy lifestyle movement. It attracts healers, has pioneered organic farms and markets, and sets high standards for foods in schools. Even in the grip of harsh income inequality dilemmas, the best of Marin County is free.

San Francisco: Pop: 788,478 **80.3%**

KH: 323,719 **DT: 62,594 [19.7%]**

If you can imagine a city population growing from 1000 to 25,000 in one year (1849), you can imagine San Francisco, a city born in a hurry with the discovery of gold. According to historical accounts, "The promise of wealth was so strong that crews on arriving vessels deserted and rushed off to the gold fields, leaving behind a forest of masts in San Francisco harbor." To this day, elegance and excess are San Francisco's twin reputations. Destroyed in 1906 by a massive earthquake and fire, idealized in the 1960s as the mecca of the Hippie movement, heartbroken in the AIDS era, overrun by tech geniuses in search of their fortunes, and finally beset by a crippling housing crisis, the city named for St. Francis is both beloved and pilloried. The legendary beauty of fog rolling in "on little cat feet..." [Carl Sandburg], cables cars and challenging hills, plus a deepfelt acceptance of the outcast are clues to the pluckiness of its residents, who continue to love San Francisco through all its changes.

New Hampshire
50.9% Blue

New Hampshire became the first colony to declare independence from Great Britain, almost six months before the Declaration of Independence was signed. The state motto "Live Free or Die" reflects its role in the American Revolutionary War, and its nickname "The Granite State" refers to the state's extensive granite formations and quarries. New Hampshire has more than 800 lakes and ponds and approximately 19,000 miles of rivers and streams; it is the state with the highest percentage of timberland growth in the country. It is a major destination for winter sports; Mount Monadnock is among the most climbed mountains in the world. Summer cottages populate the many lakes and seacoast. After the lakes freeze over, they become dotted with winter ice fishing houses, known as "Bob-houses."

The state's politics are cited as libertarian leaning. It is the least religious state, as of a 2016 Gallup poll. The Free State Project is a movement founded in 2001 to recruit at least 20,000 libertarians to move to a single low-population state. New Hampshire was selected in 2003. As of April 2022, approximately 6,232 participants have moved to New Hampshire for the Free State Project.

The following two townships voted 80% or more for Kamala Harris:

Hanover: 85%
Lyme: 84.9%

Hanover: Pop. 12,146 **85%**

KH: 6,049 **DT: 995 [13.9%]**

The town of Hanover lies along the Connecticut River, with Vermont just across the water. The White Mountains rise to the east, the Green Mountains to the west, less than an hour in either direction. In the center of town, college buildings surround the Green, home of Dartmouth College. The town was founded July 4, 1761; the college followed in 1769. "The two have grown together like vines, to the point where they're practically indistinguishable from each other," according to Annie Graves of *Yankee Magazine*. "It's a concentrated shot of culture," says one local resident. "People are well educated, and you feel it." No Republican presidential nominee has received over 40 percent of the vote in the town since George H. W. Bush in 1988.

The Appalachian Trail winds past the college-owned inn (the only inn on the 2,200 mile trail), connecting with trails and nature preserves. The majority of these trails are suitable for snowshoes and cross-country skis. Other outdoor sports abound: skating, skiing, swimming, hiking, fishing, kayaking, canoeing and camping. The Velvet Rocks Trail, located on the Appalachian Trail, has rock climbing and bouldering spots. For memorable indoor activities, the starting place might be the Hood Museum, the best free art museum in New Hampshire.

Lyme: Pop. 1,726 **84.9%**

KH: 1,050 **DT: 173 [13.9%]**

Lyme is a small rural community of just under two thousand residents situated on the eastern bank of the Connecticut River in New London County. About thirty square miles in size with a very low population density, Lyme is intensely committed to preserving its agricultural heritage and small town quality of life. Lyme residents enjoy the unspoiled beauty associated with an earlier time in New England.

Lyme is home to the Chaffee Natural Conservation Area. The Appalachian Trail passes through the town's heavily wooded eastern end. Behind the 200 year old Congregational Church is a row of horse sheds dating from 1810. This is the longest line of contiguous horse sheds in New England, and possibly in the United States.

The eastern half of the town is mostly forest. The town is home to four great ponds: Post Pond, Pout Pond, Trout Pond, and Reservoir Pond. Holts Ledge is a cliff that faces east and is part of the Dartmouth Skiway. The edge of the cliff is fenced to protect Peregrine falcons. The following warning signs are posted in the summer months:

Climbers who encounter aggressive falcons during a climb at a NH cliff should assume they are breeding close by, and are advised to immediately alter their climbing plan, and to report such encounters to New Hampshire Audubon.

New York
56.4% Blue

The history of New York begins around 10,000 BCE when the First People arrived. By 1100 CE two main cultures had become dominant, the Iroquoi and Algonqui. Both groups of natives were well-established peoples with highly sophisticated cultural systems. These were little understood or appreciated by the European colonists who encountered them. It was the Dutch in 1626 who thought they bought the colony from the Algonquian Lenape peoples, according to flimsy evidence that has become lore. In a series of wars on the continent and in the colonies, the English defeated the Dutch, and New Amsterdam was renamed New York. In the early 1700s a wave of impoverished German migrant farmers arrived and populated upstate New York.

During the 19th century, New York City was the main entry point for European immigrants, beginning with the Irish during the Great Famine. The Statue of Liberty, a gift from France officially titled "Liberty Enlightening the World," opened in 1886. Her left foot stands on a broken chain and shackle, honoring the abolition of slavery following the Civil War. The statue became an icon of freedom and of the United States, seen as a symbol of welcome to immigrants arriving by sea. Six years later, Ellis Island opened, welcoming millions more, increasingly from eastern and southern Europe.

By 1901, New York was the richest and most populous state in the U.S. Riding the tides of foreign wars, emerging social forces, and economic booms and busts, New York illuminates America's growth as a cultural and economic center. A history of immigration defines its foundation, one of embracing the refugee, integrating diversity and offering opportunity.

The following county (borough) voted over 80% for Kamala Harris:

Manhattan: 82.4%

New York County (Manhattan): Pop. 1,694,251
82.4%

KH: 533,782 **DT: 113,921 [17.4%]**

Manhattan (co-extensive with New York County) is the geographically smallest and most densely populated of the five boroughs of New York City. Known locally simply as *The City,* it is home to most of the city's skyscrapers and prominent landmarks, including Times Square and Central Park. Located almost entirely on Manhattan Island near the southern tip of the state, Manhattan is the center of the "Northeast megalopolis" and the urban core of the New York metropolitan area. New York's reputation is firmly established as an ever-evolving legend of its own making. It has been described as the cultural, financial, media, and entertainment capital of the world. The city of New York radiates a proud cosmopolitan culture, and the iconic character of the New Yorker is etched into the American psyche.

Maine
52.4% Blue

European contact with what is now called Maine started around 1200 CE when Vikings are believed to have interacted with the native Penobscot. If confirmed, this would make it the site of the earliest European discovery in America. Maine is called the Pine Tree State with over 80% of its total area forested, the most forest cover of any U.S. state.

Maine is the least densely populated state east of the Mississippi River. In the wooded areas of the interior lie much uninhabited land, some of which is not organized into formal political units, a rarity in New England. The Northwest Aroostook Unorganized Territory in the northern part of the state has an area of 2,668 square miles and a population of 10. Along the famous rock-bound coast are lighthouses, beaches, fishing villages, and thousands of offshore islands. There are jagged rocks and cliffs and many bays and inlets. Geologists describe this type of landscape as a "Drowned Coast," where a rising sea level has invaded former land features, creating bays out of valleys and islands out of mountain tops. Fishing has a long tradition in Maine. However, fish stocks largely have been depleted, and—except for lobster production—fishing has become a marginal activity.

Whites comprise virtually the entire population. The original Downeast Yankees were English and Scots-Irish Protestant immigrants who made the most substantial and perminant early settlements in Maine. They set the style of dour and taciturn industry and dry wit that is characteristic of Maine legends. Folktales, songs, local humor, and the short stories and poems of native authors are direct, earthy, and filled with a sense of the absurdity of humans' awkward attempts to subdue nature.

The following township voted 80% or more
For Kamala Harris:

Portland: 80.5%

Portland: Pop. 69, 307 80.5%

KH: 31,668 DT: 6,130 [15.6%]

Portland, seat of Cumberland County in southwestern Maine, is the state's largest city. It was named after the English Isle of Portland. (In turn, the city of Portland, Oregon, was named after Portland, Maine.) The word Portland is derived from the Old English word *Portlanda*, which means "Land surrounding a harbor." Portland is becoming increasingly affected by global warming and the rise of sea levels. The coast is one of the fastest-warming saltwater bodies. It is predicted to see an increase to 10—17 inches by 2030, in comparison to the levels in 2000. In 2022, the National Oceanic and Atmospheric Administration issued a report that showed sea level in Portland could rise by six inches by 2050, two feet by 2060 and two to six feet by 2100.

Fires and floods have left their imprint on Portland and its hardy residents. A fire that resulted from an Independence Day celebration destroyed much of the city center in 1866. In a commemorative edition published in 2016, *The Portland News Herald* reported that "As the sun rose on July 5, one of the most beautiful cities in the union had been reduced to smoldering piles of rubble." The burning of Portland led to a new national system for assessing fire risk that still exists today. On January 13, 2024, torrential rains combined with an astronomical high tide. High winds raised 15 foot waves and set records for flooding. Iconic fishermen's shacks floated away in the surge.

In calmer times, Portland enjoys a national reputation for the quality of its restaurants, eateries, festivals and food culture. *Bon Appetit* named Portland the Restaurant City of the Year in 2018. In 2018, the Portland City Council banned the use of synthetic pesticides, and the city requires organic land care techniques be used on both public and private property. Sebago Lake is one of fifty surface water supplies among 13,000 in the country that the Environmental Protection Agency says do not need filtration. In 2013 Portland voters overwhelmingly approved an ordinance to legalize the possession and private use of cannabis for adults, making the city the first municipality in the Eastern United States to do so.

The 20 Blue States of 2024

State and % for Kamala Harris:		KH votes:	DT votes:
Washington, D.C.	92.5%	294,185	21,076
Vermont	64.4%	235,185	119,395
Maryland	63%	1,894,27	1,033,899
Massachusetts	61.6%	2,126,545	1,251,308
Hawaii	60.6%	313,044	193,661
California	58.5%	9,275,051	6,080,485
Washington	57.6%	2,245,849	1,530,923
Delaware	56.6%	289,758	214,351
New York	56.4%	4,583,210	3,548,552
Connecticut	56.4%	994,287	739,317
Oregon	55.6%	1,228,410	910,702
Rhode Island	55%	285,156	214,406
Illinois	54.8%	3,056,367	2,444,631
Maine	52.4%	435,584	376,231
Colorado	54.2%	1,728,159	1,377,441
Virginia	52.1%	2,335,395	2,075,085
New Jersey	52%	2,220,662	1,968,212
New Mexico	51.9%	478,802	423,391
Minnesota	51.1%	1,656,979	1,519,032
New Hampshire	50.9%	418,496	395,579

State Animals

Massachusetts:
Right whale

California:
California grizzly bear

Virginia:
Virginia big-eared bat

Vermont:
Morgan horse

Maine:
Moose

Connecticut:
Sperm whale

Washington, D.C.:
Big brown bat

New York:
North American beaver

Maryland:
Thoroughbread horse

New Hampshire:
White-tailed deer

"WHEREFORE, instead of gazing at each other with suspicious or doubtful curiosity, let each of us hold out to his neighbor the hearty hand of friendship, and unite in drawing a line, which, like an act of oblivion, shall bury in forgetfulness every former dissension. Let names of Whig and Tory be extinct; and let none other be heard among us, than those of a good citizen, an open and resolute friend, and a virtuous supporter of the RIGHTS of MANKIND, and of the FREE AND INDEPENDENT STATES OF AMERICA..."

-Thomas Payne, *Common Sense*, 1776

Common Sense, 2025

As I worked on this book, the background noise has been the daily events of the newly elected presidency. The words "coup" and "fascist" and "unprecedented" are written and spoken routinely now at all levels of media. We find ourselves living in a reality that belongs in a fictional movie, not on the PBS News Hour. People may say they saw it coming, but that's like saying we saw the category five hurricane coming because it was drawn on a weather map. The physical reality of the hurricane is a different creature all together. We are dealing with a constitutional crisis with an unknown outcome.

There are lessons to be learned from living through massive disruptions, like floods, storms, and wildfires–all of which are also occurring. When the norms are overwhelmed, living in the present is a no longer a nice idea, it's a necessity. In the center of the storm, there is calm and an opportunity to reorganize and cope. This is the place where we can join together and find inspiration. It is the source of our common sense.

Political commentary on how this all came to be is the most useless use of our intelligence. Inevitably, one candidate was going to win, and one candidate was going to lose, like the World Series. Why speculate, analyze, and hypothesize? For most of us, the leap to Kamala Harris came out of nowhere. Who could have predicted that bullet in Butler, Pennsylvania? You could say it was a *deus ex machina,* a classical Greek plot device to shake things up through the intervention of the gods. It pushed the plot into a further unfolding, and that is where we are now. Metaphysically speaking, that is also where we are meant to be. The story is unfolding, and it is ripe for our involvement.

Our system of government is under assault, and it will unlikely never bounce back to the old norms, no matter what the midterms bring. We have been trying to mix the government of money and the government of moral purpose for too long, and these two just don't want to mix. They want to fight. Right now, the money forces have effectively stormed the castle of government. They're drunk with power, and they think themselves invincible. Their hubris is going to be their undoing, but we don't know how or when.

Meanwhile, we must find the calm center within ourselves and collectively. I'm suggesting that it is in these strongholds of moral purpose symbolized by the 80% vote that we will find this place of renewal. Of course it can be anywhere; the 80% is a way to imagine it, a way to start the discussion.

I'm not naively stating that all Democrats are good and all Republicans are bad, because that is not what I believe. In the 2024 election campaign we witnessed an ominous threat to our system from a force that is willing to create great harm to many innocent people. This force orchestrated a campaign to present itself as a savior in a time of general distress and anxiety, and it gained the power it needed to succeed. It did it through the hypnotic power of imagining money as savior, capturing the projections of the haves and the have-nots alike. It was the culmination of a long plan to merge the institutions of money into the institutions of social organization and take them over in perpetuity.

Now we are in phase two. It is not ordinary politics anymore, although that game is still floundering around in habitual ways. It is a time when we must once again reach deeply into the issues and inspiration of the first American Revolution, issues that inspired Thomas Paine to write his harangue against the King of England. Paine called for a "Continental Congress" of elected representatives because in his time it was clear the colonists were identifying themselves not with England but with the promise of a new and unique continental homeland.

To be sure, his vision was not expansive enough to see the criminality and cruelty that the colonial culture was inflicting on Native Peoples. Undoing this terrible ignorance is our legacy. It is intertwined with ignoring the suffering perpetrated on immigrants and asylum seekers. The promise of our homeland is corrupted when we marginalize anyone as not worthy of being treated as welcome, especially those who belonged here long before us.

Let us try again to form a coalition of like-minded individuals to envision how we protect our democracy from this insurgence and restructure our social institutions to meet the reality of today. Everyone knows that the root problem of our world, not just our country, is the ability of wealth to corrupt absolutely. What is the cure for that disease? Lots of utopias have tried to work on that and failed. What keeps us from sharing? Is it a moral failing? Is it spiritual emptiness? Is it psychological trauma? Is it a cosmic dispensation?

These are the discussions that need to take place in the calm center of the storm we are witnessing. The invitation to participate must include the respected and the neglected, the outliers and the insiders, the elders of the First Peoples, spiritual masters and visionaries, women, youth, and the marginalized. Everyone. When the circle is whole, there will be transformation.

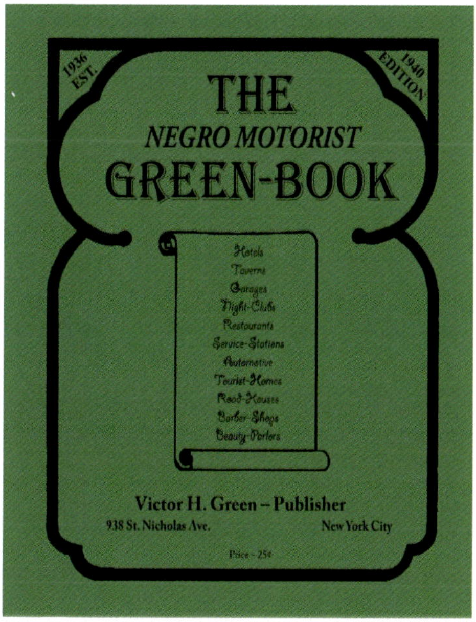

About the Author and *The American Blue Book*

The Negro Motorist Green-Book is the inspiration for the cover design of *The American Blue Book*. It was published for 30 years (1936-1967) as a guidebook for African-American travelers seeking safe and friendly businesses in the tense era of segregation. Developed by Victor Hugo Green, a Black mail carrier in Harlem, New York, it listed accommodations, restaurants, service businesses and tourist attractions run by Black owners, opening up safe travel to families in the early days of the automobile. It quickly became an essential guide.

Elizabeth Whitney is a fifth-generation Californian, born in San Francisco. She spent her teenage years in Berkeley in the 1950s as the Civil Rights movement was making headlines. Her family was politically active and aware, so political conversations were always in the air, particularly in the McCarthy era. The daughter of a journalist and foreign correspondent, she also took to journalism from a young age. After graduating from Scripps college in Claremont, California, she headed for Washington, D.C. and joined the staff at the *Washington Star*. Subsequent metro newspaper jobs followed in New York and Oakland. In the early 1970s, she returned to coastal Marin County, California, and the summer vacation town of her childhood and her two grandmothers.

In 1976 a band of creatives started an alternative newspaper called the *Tomales Bay Times*, and Elizabeth served as its editor. Alternative publishing thrived in the 1970s and 1980s, and she innovated and published various short-lived but well-loved newspapers and newsletters that came and went: The *West Coast News*, *The New Weather Observer*, *The Inverness Daily News* flood emergency newspaper, *The Tidelines Express*, *Mercury Renegade*, and *The Timebandit*. Over the years she also wrote columns for several weekly publications that have also come and gone: *The Great Western Coastal Post*, *The Malibu Surfside News*, and *The West Marin Citizen.*

While the era of print journalism was surrendering to television and ultimately to the present day mélange of social media, podcasts, videos and blogs, she continued political activism on several fronts, participating in six major civil disobedience actions. Her interests extended into metaphysical explorations, Mayan prophecy, Aikido, and studies influenced by Carl Jung, Chögyam Trungpa, and Jose Arguelles. Books on politics, art, mythology, mysticism, quantum theory, cosmology, natural time, and classical religion co-exist on her bookshelves, testimonies to her lifelong quest to understand such questions as "Why do we have the world we have when nobody wants it this way?"

As an elder, Elizabeth sees the current political crisis in America through a long lens. Good and bad times come and go in cycles, some as short as four years based on the presidential electoral process and some as aspects of grand galactic timing rhythms. Individuals have roles to play within all these seasons, as personal destinies within larger evolutionary cycles. Each one is a fractal of the big picture, and each one is essential. Every unique human, using free will, has a part to play, a destiny to reveal, and a contribution to the whole. This is the spirit in which *The American Blue Book* is offered.

Order *The American Blue Book*:

Individual books: $15.00
Books in quantity:
- 6 books .... $75.00 ($15 discount)
- 10 books.........$125.00 ($25 discount)
- 20 books.........$225.00 ($75 discount)

Bookstores are welcome to inquire about consignment and wholesale distribution options. If a local group wants to order and sell *The American Blue Book* for fundraising, please inquire about larger quantities. Shipping and sales tax will be added to the order where applicable. Please pay by cash, check or money order. Make checks payable to Tomales Bay Times Publications:

Tomales Bay Times Publications
P.O. Box 894, Point Reyes Station CA, 94956
www.tomalesbaytimes.com